Build-a-Skill Instant Books

Synonyms and Antonyms

Written by
Kim Cernek and Rozanne Lanczak Williams

Editor: Stacey Faulkner
Illustrator: Jenny Campbell
Cover Illustrator: Rick Grayson
Designer: The Development Source
Art Director: Moonhee Pak
Project Director: Betsy Morris

Printed in China through Colorcraft Ltd., Hong Kong

Table of Contents

Synonym Instant Books

Antonym Instant Books

Introduction

About the Build-a-Skill Instant Books Series

The *Build-a-Skill Instant Books* series features a variety of reproducible instant books that focus on important reading and math skills covered in the primary classroom. Each instant book is easy to make, and once children become familiar with the basic formats that appear throughout the series, they will be able to make new books with little help. Children will love the unique, manipulative quality of the books and will want to read them over and over again as they gain mastery of basic learning skills!

About the Build-a-Skill Instant Books: Synonyms and Antonyms

This book features commonly used and easy-to-read synonyms and antonyms in fun and easy-to-make instant books. Children will develop fine motor skills and practice following directions as they cut, fold, and staple the reproducible pages together to make flip books, strip books, mini books, and more! As children read and reread their instant books, they will improve their understanding of synonyms and antonyms, and increase their vocabulary.

Refer to the Table of Contents to help with lesson planning. Choose instant book activities that fit with current curriculum goals in your regular or ELL classroom. Use the instant books to practice skills or introduce new ones. Directions for making the instant books appear on pages 3 and 4. These should be copied and sent along with the book patterns when assigning a bookmaking activity as homework.

Making and Using the Instant Books

Most of the instant books in this resource require only one or two pieces of paper. Copy the pages on white copy paper or card stock, or use colored paper to jazz up and vary the formats. Children will love personalizing their instant books by coloring them, adding construction paper covers, or decorating them with collage materials such as wiggly eyes, ribbon, and stickers. Customize the instant books by adding extra pages, or by creating your own synonym and antonym cards using the reproducible on page 14.

Children can make instant books as an enrichment activity when their regular classwork is done, as a learning center activity during guided reading time, or as a homework assignment. They can place completed instant books in their classroom book boxes and then read and reread the books independently or with a reading buddy. After children have had many opportunities to read their books in school, send the books home for extra skill-building practice. Encourage children to store the books in a special box that they have labeled "I Can Read Box."

Directions for Making the Instant Books

There are five basic formats for the instant books in this guide. The directions appear below for quick and easy reference. The directions are written *to* the child, in case you would like to send the bookmaking activities home as homework. Just copy the directions and attach them to the instant book pages.

To have children practice identifying synonyms and antonyms, use the word cards on pages 8–13 with the instant books on pages 5–7. As a rule of thumb, six to ten cards can be easily stapled onto each instant book. To have children practice synonyms and antonyms in context, use the instant books on pages 15–32.

Synonym Flip Books, page 5

1. Cut out the two flip books, synonym word cards, and blank word cards.
2. Sort the synonym word cards into pairs.
3. Staple the word card pairs to the "I can read synonyms" flip book.
4. Staple the blank word cards to the "I can write synonyms" flip book.
5. Practice reading and writing pairs of synonyms!

Antonym Flip Books, page 6

1. Cut out the two flip books, antonym word cards, and blank word cards.
2. Sort the antonym word cards into pairs.
3. Staple the word card pairs to the "I can read antonyms" flip book.
4. Staple the blank word cards to the "I can write antonyms" flip book.
5. Practice reading and writing pairs of antonyms!

Read-and-Write Book, page 7

1. Cut out the read-and-write book.
2. Glue it to a piece of construction paper the same size.
3. Cut out the word cards and sort them into pairs.
4. Staple the word card pairs to the top strip.
5. Fold the book in half and decorate the cover.
6. Practice reading and writing your word pairs!

Strip Book, pages 15, 18, 22, 24, 25, 27, 29, and 31

1. Finish the book by writing the words.
2. Cut out the strips.
3. Put the strips in order. Staple them on the left.

Optional: Make and decorate a construction paper cover, and color the pictures.

Word Wallet, pages 16–17, 20–21

1. Cut out the wallet.
2. Fold it in half along the solid middle line.
3. Staple where shown. Tape the outer edges. Fold the wallet closed.
4. Cut out the word cards. Sort them into the correct pockets.

Mini Book, pages 19, 23, 26, 28, 30, and 32

1. Finish the book by tracing and/or writing the words.
2. Cut along the solid lines to make four pages.
3. Put the pages in order. Staple them on the left.

Optional: Make and decorate a construction paper cover, and color the pictures

Synonym Flip Books

I can read synonyms.

Staple word cards here.

I can write synonyms.

Staple word cards here.

Antonym Flip Books

I can read antonyms.

Staple word cards here.

I can write antonyms.

Staple word cards here.

Read-and-Write Book

Staple word cards here.

I can read

I can write

Synonym Word Cards

Synonyms are words that mean the same thing.	big	large
ill	sick	mix
stir	small	little

Synonym Word Cards

laugh	giggle	fast
quick	hot	warm
cold	cool	happy

Synonym Word Cards

glad	mad	angry
hop	jump	kind
nice	loud	noisy

Antonym Word Cards

Antonyms are words that have the opposite meaning.	big	small
short	tall	yes
no	fast	slow

Antonym Word Cards

hot	cold	over
under	up	down
first	last	in

Antonym Word Cards

out	hard	soft
on	off	empty
full	stop	go

Make Your Own

Word Cards

Synonym Strip Book

Words That Mean the Same

Another word for **big** is __________.

Another word for **ill** is __________.

1

Another word for **laugh** is __________.

Another word for **fast** is __________.

2

Another word for **hot** is __________.

Another word for **sport** is __________.

3

Another word for **cool** is __________.

Synonyms are words that mean the same!

4

quick giggle warm cold game sick large

Synonym Word Wallet

Wallet Words: Synonyms

gloomy	glad	cross
cheerful	unhappy	crabby
angry	down	joyful

Synonym Strip Book

My Cat Tabbi

My cat Tabbi is too __________.
(skinny)

1

So, I'm glad when she __________
(chomps)
her food.

2

It's fun to watch her __________
(jump)
on her toy.

3

Tabbi is so __________.
(cute)
She is the best pet ever!

4

pounce thin adorable munches

Synonym Mini Book

Synonym Word Wallet

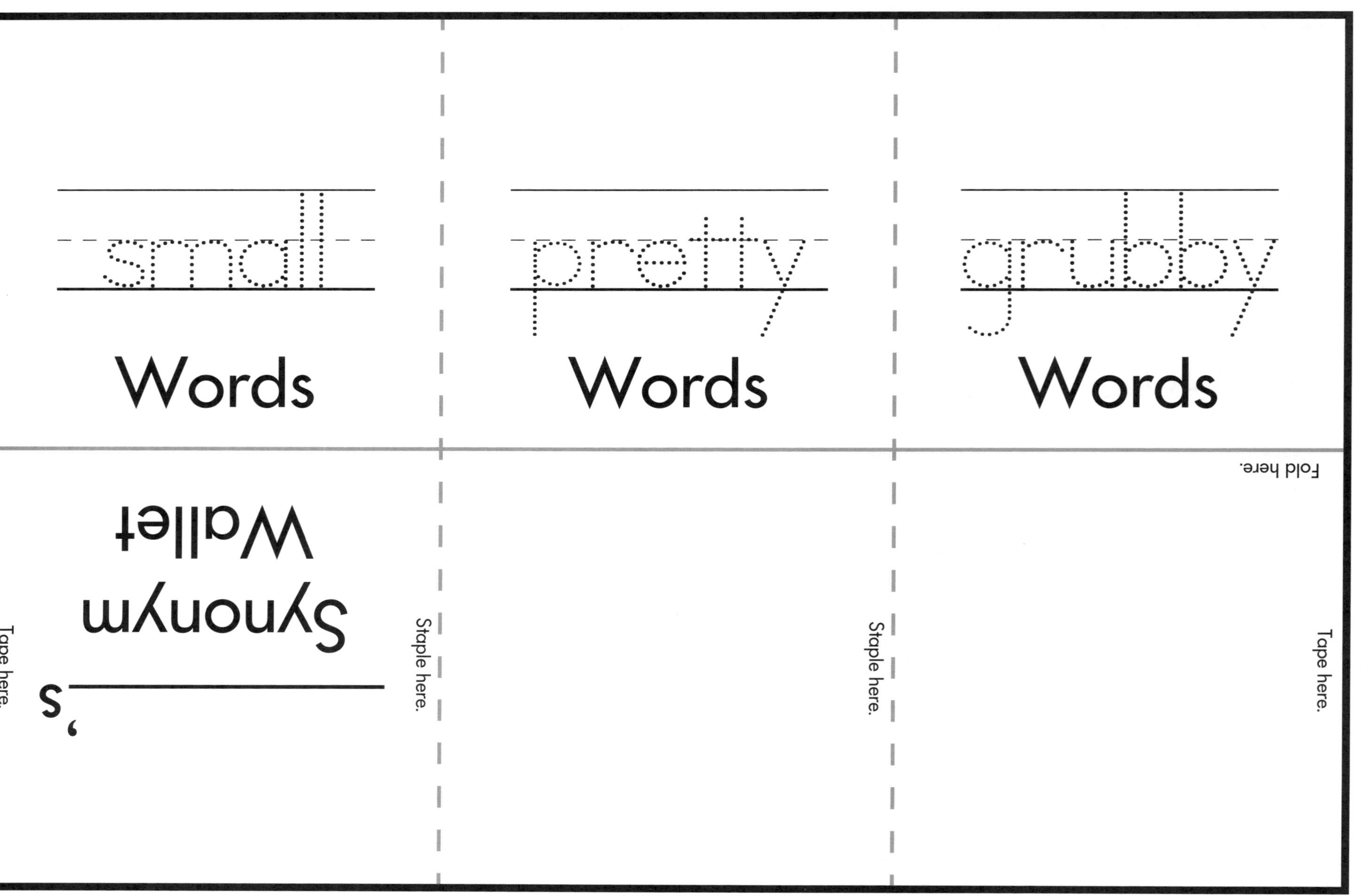

Wallet Words: Synonyms

filthy	beautiful	dirty
little	lovely	itty-bitty
tiny	grimy	cute

Synonym Strip Book

________________________'s

Synonym Poem 1

When I'm **sluggish** I am ___________.

When I **leave**, that means I ___________. 2

An **amusing** story is ___________.

A **bright** day outside is ___________. 3

A **male** is a ___________.

An **idea** is a ___________. 4

Synonyms are fun!

Can you think of some? 5

go plan funny man slow sunny

Synonym Mini Book

Antonym Strip Book

Antonyms Are Opposites

___________'s Book

1

The opposite of **short** is __________.

The opposite of **big** is __________.

2

The opposite of **dirty** is __________.

The opposite of **nice** is __________.

3

The opposite of **yes** is __________.

The opposite of **fast** is __________.

4

The opposite of **many** is __________.

Learning antonyms is fun to do!

5

slow mean tall few no clean small

Antonym Strip Book

Hot or Cold?

________________'s Book

1

The sun is __________.

2

The sidewalk is __________.

3

My dog is __________.

4

My cat is __________.

5

But my ice cream is __________! M-m-m-m!

6

Antonym Mini Book

Antonym Strip Book

Storybook Opposites

1

Granny was ______________.

The wolf was ______________.

2

Humpty sat __________ a wall.

Humpty fell __________ a wall.

3

The goats went __________ the bridge.

The troll sat ______________ it.

4

over mean on under nice off

Antonym Mini Book

Antonym Strip Book

______________________'s

Antonym Poem

1

The opposite of **left** is __________.

The opposite of **dull** is __________.

2

The opposite of **work** is __________.

The opposite of **night** is __________.

3

The opposite of **false** is __________.

The opposite of **many** is __________.

4

I can write antonyms. How about you?

5

true bright few day right play

Antonym Mini Book

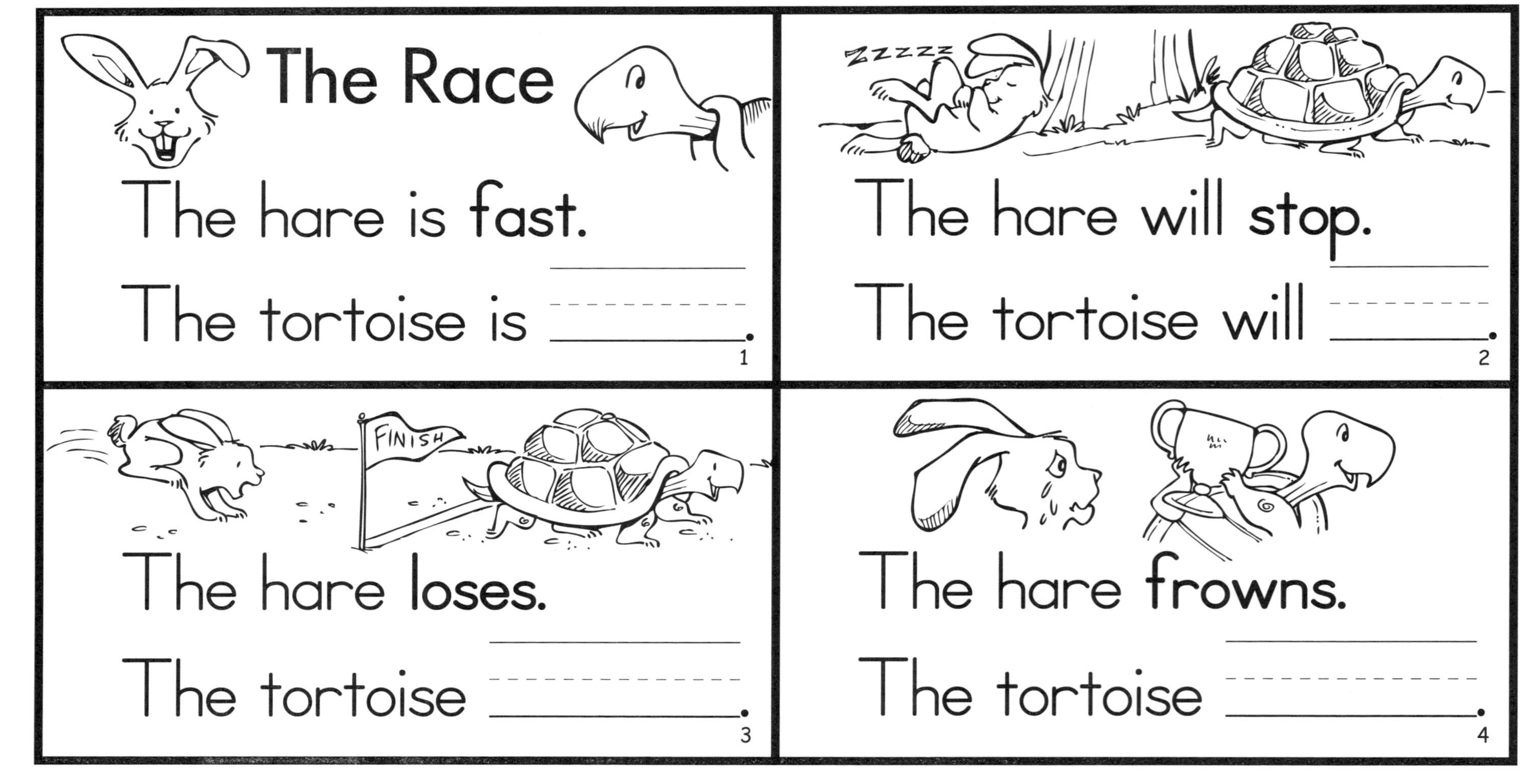

wins slow grins go

Antonym Strip Book

_______________'s Opposites

When I'm not going **up**,

I'm going __________.

1

When I don't have a **smile**,

I have a __________.

2

When I'm not being **sloppy**,

I'm being __________.

3

When I **lose** a tooth,

then I __________ a treat!

4

frown find down neat

Antonym Mini Book

________'s

Best and Worst

1

The **best** food

____

is ________.

The **worst** food

____

is ________.

2

The **best** weather

____

is ________.

The **worst** weather

____

is ________.

3

The **best** day ever is

____

________.

4